I know a Fox With Dirty Socks

77 very easy, very little songs for beginners

for singing and playing

by William Starr

I know a fox
with dirt - y socks

© 2006 Summy-Birchard Music
division of Summy-Birchard Inc.
Exclusive print rights administered by
Alfred Music Publishing Co., Inc.
All rights reserved

ISBN-10: 0-7390-4120-7
ISBN-13: 978-0-7390-4120-8

Contents

Dotted-Quarter and Eighth-Note Rhythms

Low 1st and Low 4th Finger Patterns

Fast Finger Action

Preface

When is she going to play a song?

Now! After she sings it first!

A song in the ear is easy to play!

If she can sing it, she can play it!

Students learn songs more quickly than they learn tunes.

Students remember songs better than they remember tunes.

These 77 little songs are easy and fun to play

23 songs have "giggle" words.

Some have familiar words and tunes.

Graded according to finger patterns, and bowings.

A great help through the periods of boredom and frustration.

Supplement Suzuki books or public school materials.

Singable songs improve ear and memory.

For group or private teaching.

A new piece each lesson.

Duet parts for teacher or students

GET OUR STRINGS TO SING!

I know a fox
with dirt - y socks

Suggestions for Use

Private or group lessons

1. Teach these songs by rote, in small units (suggested divisions are marked in the music).

2. Sing the song, or play it saying the words, and then ask the student to sing with you. Student may look at the words.

3. Make sure the student can sing the song, or part of it before trying to play it. Student should not look at the music while playing.

4. Demonstrate the fingering and bowing, then play in unison with the student.

5. Feel free to teach these songs in your own order.

6. Do not teach a song the student dislikes. There are plenty of songs!

7. After a few songs are learned with the first finger pattern, skip to a few string-crossing songs, then to the songs using the second finger pattern.

8. Add the harmony part only when it will not disturb the beginner.

9. Use these songs to introduce a new technique, then repeat often, improving the technique with repetitions.

Group Lesson Games

1. Divide class in half.
   A) one half plays, the other half sings.
   B) one half plays or sings, the other half claps the rhythm.

2. Play memory games in sing-a-longs.

3. Later ... class plays the songs, reading the music.

4. Later ... class plays both parts from the music.

1. I Know a Fox - with Dirty Socks

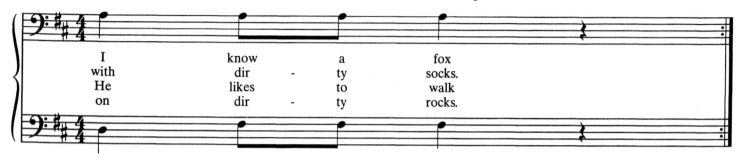

2. Old Sea Turtles

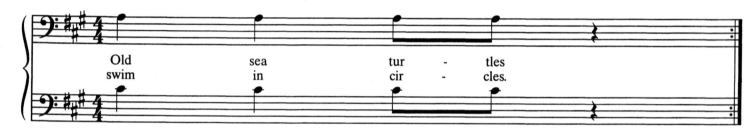

3. I Like Green Frogs

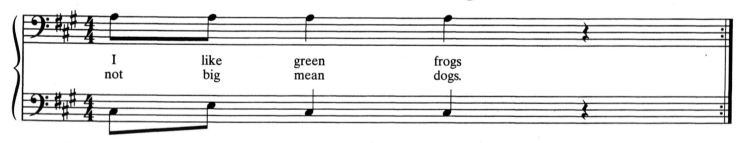

4. Big Green Avocados

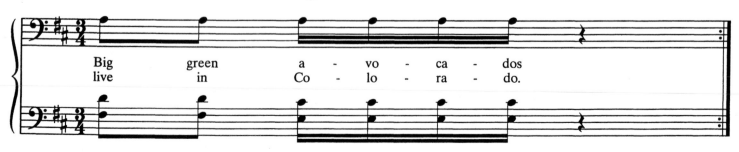

5. Little Miss Muffet

Lit - tle Miss Muf - fet,   sat   on   a   pup - pet.

6. Baby in the Bed

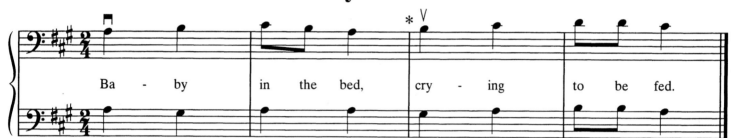

Ba - by   in   the   bed,   cry - ing   to   be   fed.

7. Sam's Box

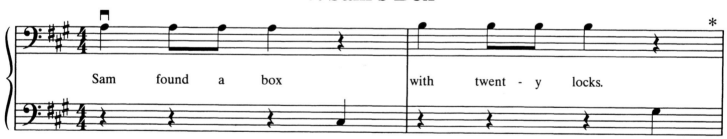

Sam   found   a   box   with   twent - y   locks.

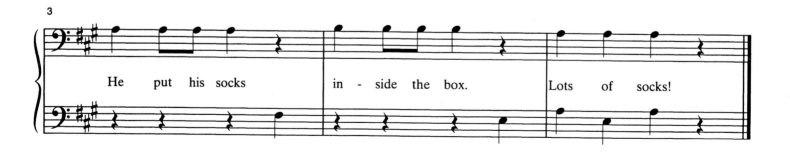

He   put   his   socks   in - side   the   box.   Lots   of   socks!

8. Oh No

9. The Moonlight

10. Hot Cross Buns

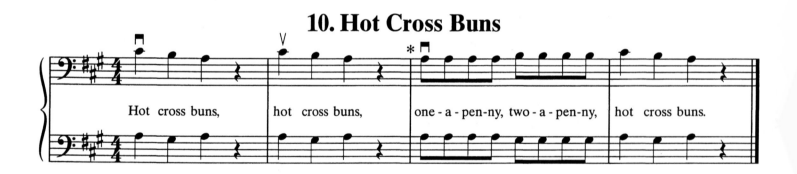

11. Cuckoo

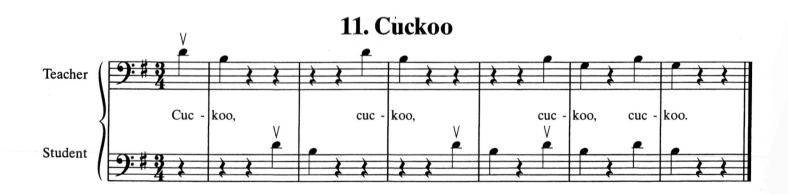

12. Mary Had a Little Lamb

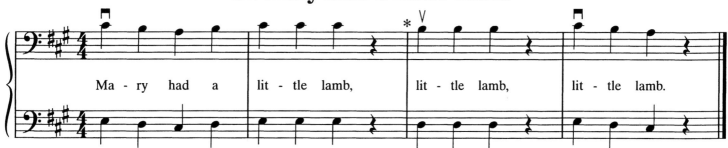

13. Japanese Folk Song

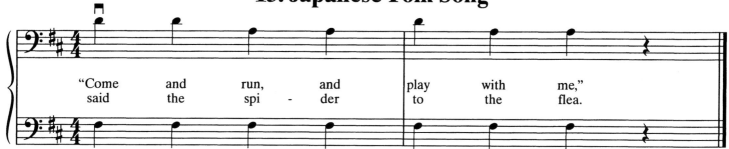

14. The Goofy Donkey

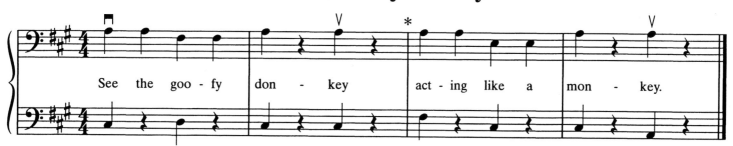

15. Nonsense Song

16. Jack Sprat

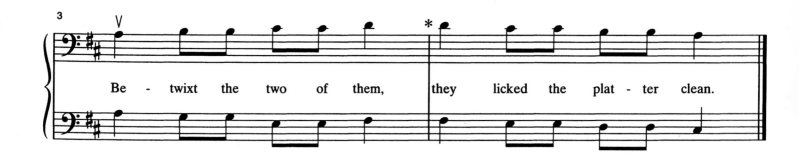

Jack Sprat could eat no fat, his wife could eat no lean.

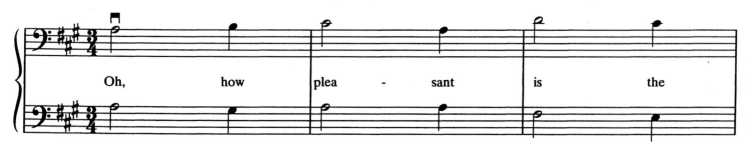

Be - twixt the two of them, they licked the plat - ter clean.

17. Oh, How Pleasant

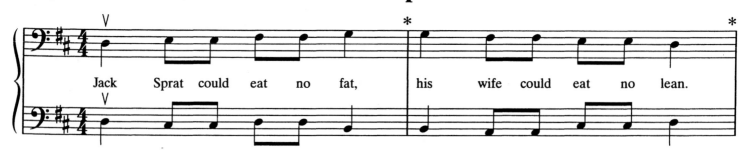

Oh, how plea - sant is the

eve - ning, is the eve - ning.

18. One Little Frog

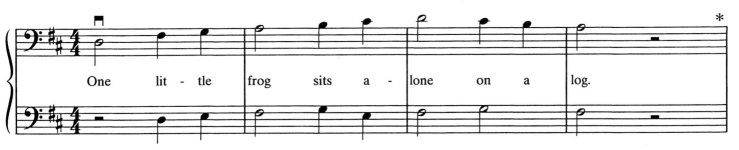

One lit - tle frog sits a - lone on a log.

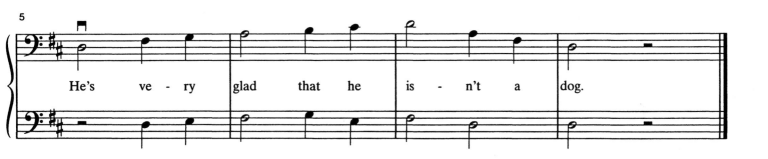

He's ve - ry glad that he is - n't a dog.

19. Can You Not See

Can you not see? We're the same you and me!

20. Winter is Coming

The win - ter is com - ing and aut - umn is turn - ing the leaves.

21. String Crossing Song

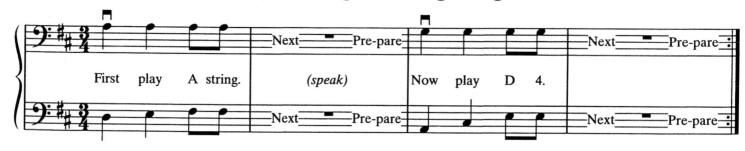

22. Old MacDonald

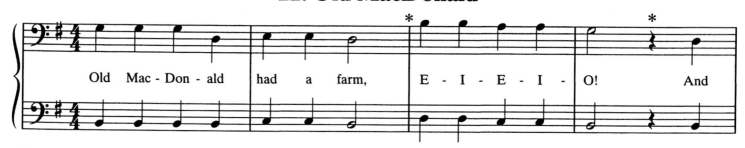

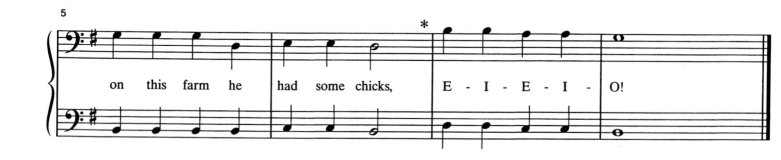

23. Sleep, Baby, Sleep

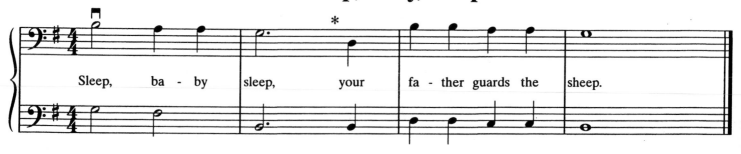

24. Monkeys Swinging

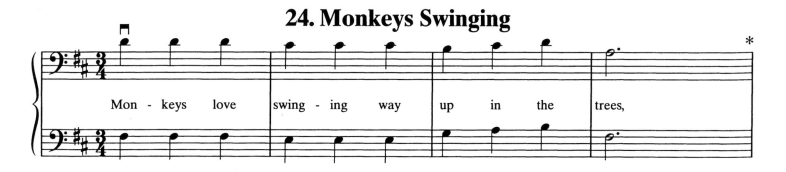

Mon - keys love swing - ing way up in the trees,

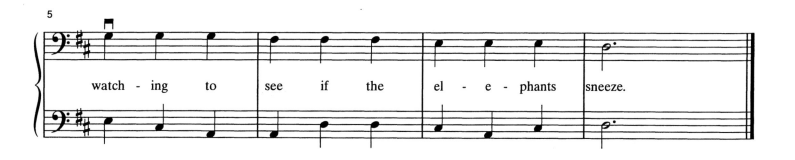

watch - ing to see if the el - e - phants sneeze.

25. Baa, Baa, Black Sheep

Baa, Baa, black sheep, have you a - ny wool? Yes sir, yes sir, three bags full.

26. Jack and Jill

Jack and Jill went up the hill to fetch a pail of wa - ter,

Jack fell down and broke his crown and Jill came tum - bling af - ter.

14

27. Joyful Song

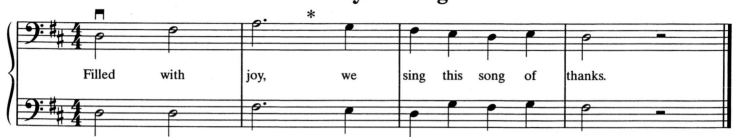

Filled with joy, we sing this song of thanks.

28. Tabby Cat

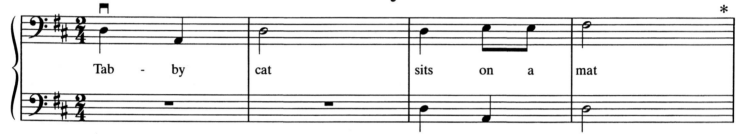

Tab - by cat sits on a mat

5

and wears a hat. That is that.

29. The Rabbit Runs

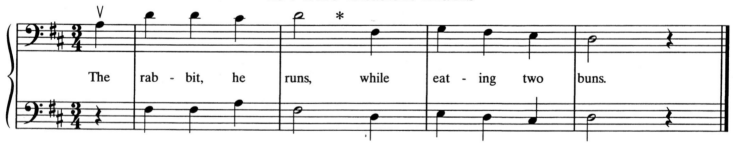

The rab - bit, he runs, while eat - ing two buns.

30. Jingle Bells

Jin - gle bells, jin - gle bells, jin - gle all the way.

31. A-running, A-running

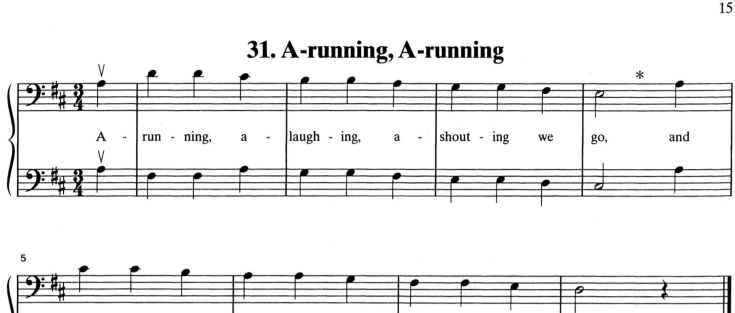

A - run - ning, a - laugh - ing, a - shout - ing we go, and

sli - ding, and slip - ping and fall - ing in snow.

32. Polly, Dolly

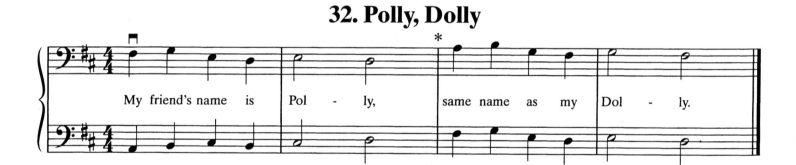

My friend's name is Pol - ly, same name as my Dol - ly.

33. Merrily We Roll Along

Mer - ri - ly, we roll a - long, roll a - long, roll a - long.

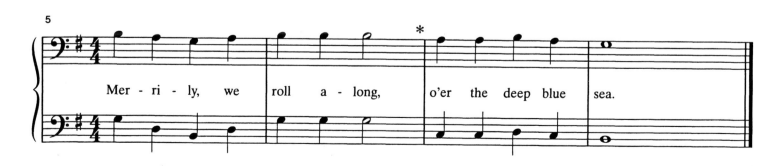

Mer - ri - ly, we roll a - long, o'er the deep blue sea.

16

34. Little Mary

Lit - tle Ma - ry found a frog, it was sit - ting on a log.

35. Jane Goes Up

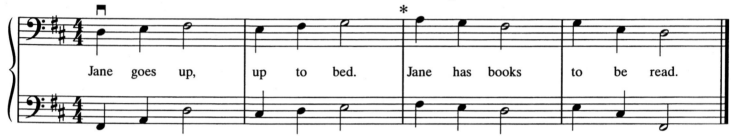

Jane goes up, up to bed. Jane has books to be read.

36. Sue Ran Up the Stairs

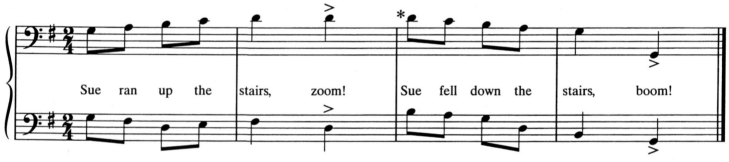

Sue ran up the stairs, zoom! Sue fell down the stairs, boom!

37. Joyful, Joyful

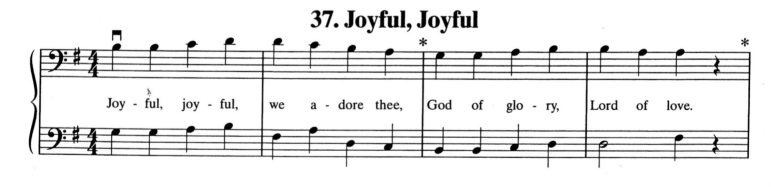

Joy - ful, joy - ful, we a - dore thee, God of glo - ry, Lord of love.

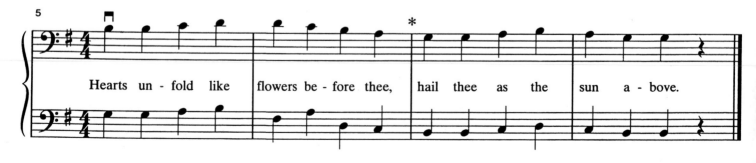

Hearts un - fold like flowers be - fore thee, hail thee as the sun a - bove.

Mostly 1-2-4 Finger Patterns

38. Start Song

39. Papa Haydn

40. Smashed Cross Buns

41. Zum Gali

42. Peas Porridge Hot

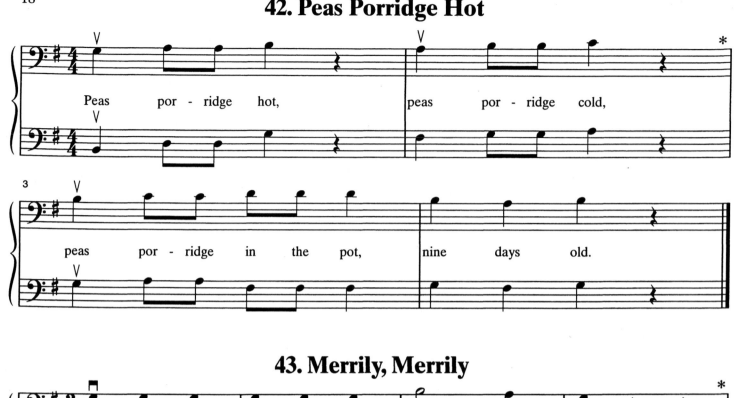

Peas por - ridge hot, peas por - ridge cold,

peas por - ridge in the pot, nine days old.

43. Merrily, Merrily

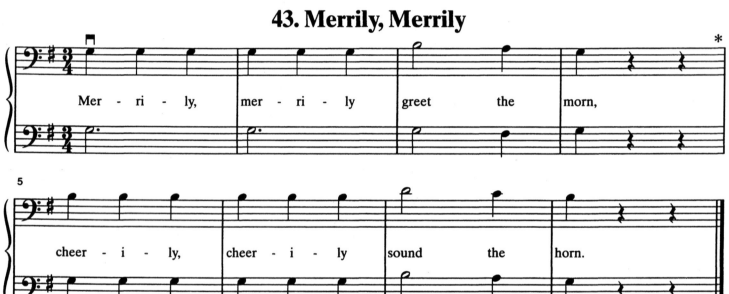

Mer - ri - ly, mer - ri - ly greet the morn,

cheer - i - ly, cheer - i - ly sound the horn.

44. Simple Simon

Sim - ple Si - mon met a pie - man, go - ing to the fair, says

sim - ple Si - mon to the pie - man, "Let me taste your ware."

45. Two Little Foxes

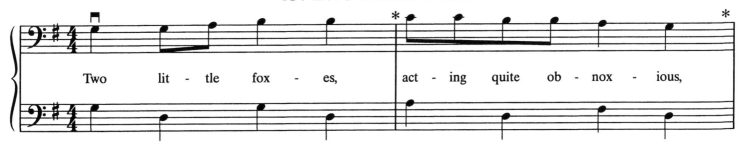

Two lit - tle fox - es, act - ing quite ob - nox - ious,

they're on - ly good boys when their moth - er watch - es.

46. Everybody Likes a Treat

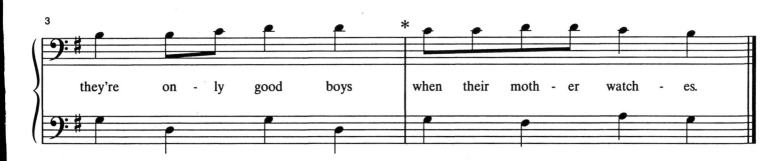

Ever - y - bod - y likes a treat when they have shoes on their feet.

47. Time For Practicing

Run and play, dance and sing, when your play is ov - er, time for prac - ti - cing.

20

48. Ding-dong Song

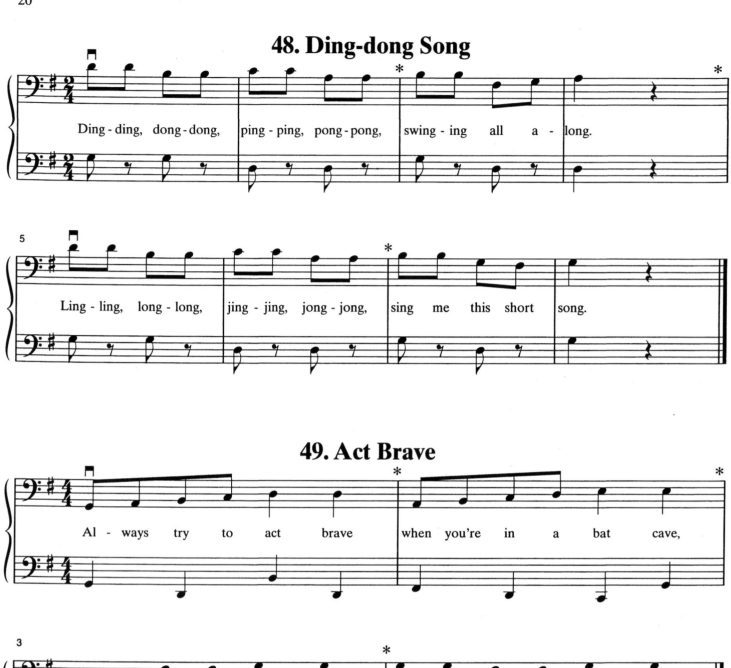

Ding - ding, dong - dong, ping - ping, pong - pong, swing - ing all a - long.

Ling - ling, long - long, jing - jing, jong - jong, sing me this short song.

49. Act Brave

Al - ways try to act brave when you're in a bat cave,

or you're fac - ing big waves, al - ways try to act brave.

50. Spring Has Arrived

The spring has ar - rived and plants are a - live.

51. Fiddle, Middle

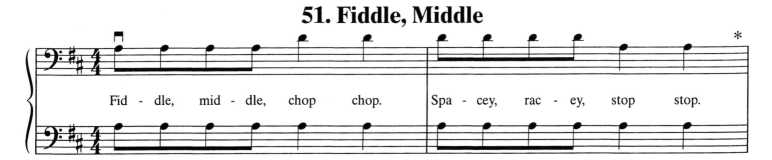

Fid - dle, mid - dle, chop chop. Spa - cey, rac - ey, stop stop.

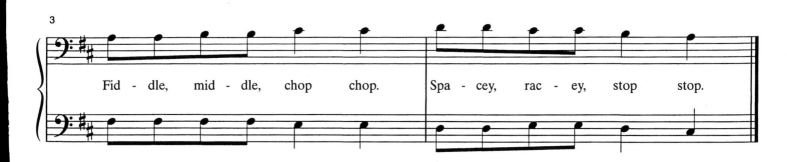

Fid - dle, mid - dle, chop chop. Spa - cey, rac - ey, stop stop.

52. Driving in a Cool Car

Driv - ing in a cool car does - n't make a rock star,

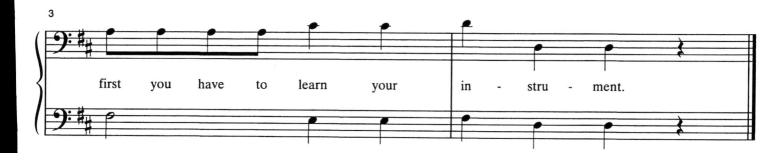

first you have to learn your in - stru - ment.

53. Jack and the Candlestick

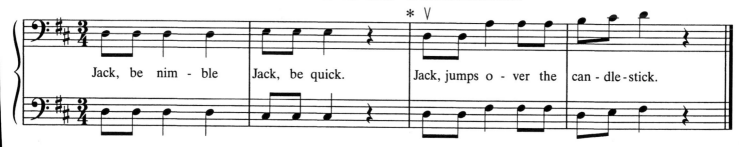

Jack, be nim - ble Jack, be quick. Jack, jumps o - ver the can - dle-stick.

22

54. On the Bridge of Avignon

On the bridge of A - vi - gnon, there is danc - ing all a - round.

55. Maoz Tzur

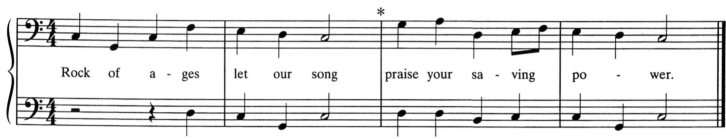

Rock of a - ges let our song praise your sa - ving po - wer.

56. If Gold Can Turn

If gold can turn to glue or zinc,
then pigs can fly and blue is pink.

57. Singing Fifty Songs

I'll sing you fif - ty songs, Sus - ie, I'll sing you fif - ty songs, Sus - ie, I'll

5

sing you fif - ty songs, Sus - ie, all through the long, long night, dear.

58. Little Tommy Tucker

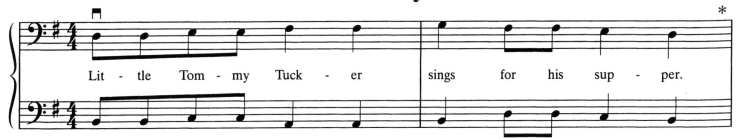

Lit - tle Tom - my Tuck - er sings for his sup - per.

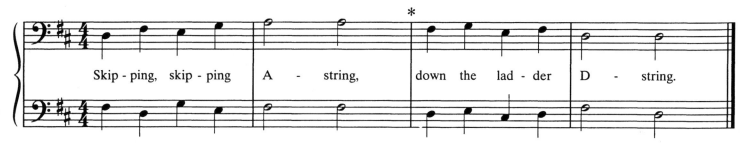

What shall he eat? White bread and but - ter.

59. Skipping

Skip - ping, skip - ping A - string, down the lad - der D - string.

60. Alligators

Al - li - ga - tors swim - ming in a mur - ky swamp,

care - ful of your fin - gers 'cause they might get chomped.

61. Dear Brahms

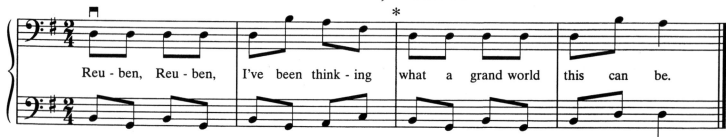

Dear Brahms wrote this beau - ti - ful me - lo - dy for us.

62. Reuben, Reuben

Reu - ben, Reu - ben, I've been think - ing what a grand world this can be.

63. Welcome Song

Wel - come to the fest - iv - al, run, dance, have your fun.

When the fest - iv - al is done, sleep well my tir - ed son.

64. Ted

Ted wants to go back to bed. He has a bump on his head.

65. Counting Song

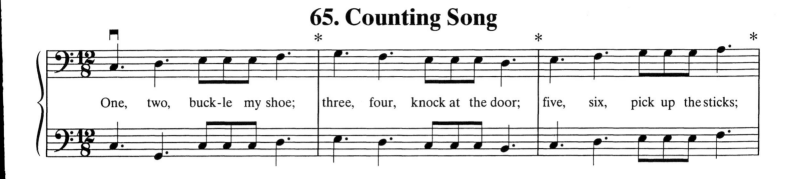

One, two, buck-le my shoe; three, four, knock at the door; five, six, pick up the sticks;

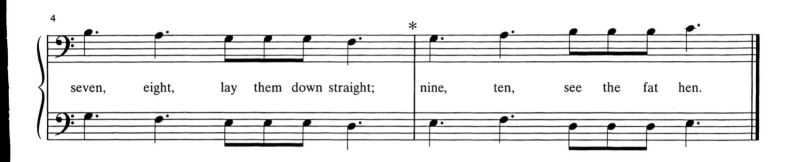

seven, eight, lay them down straight; nine, ten, see the fat hen.

66. Fiddle-dee-dee

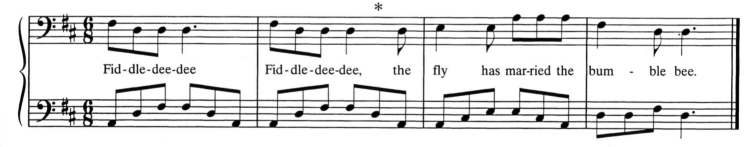

Fid-dle-dee-dee Fid-dle-dee-dee, the fly has mar-ried the bum - ble bee.

67. O Come, All Ye Faithful

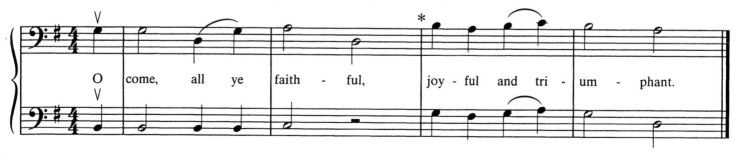

O come, all ye faith - ful, joy - ful and tri - um - phant.

68. Deck the Halls

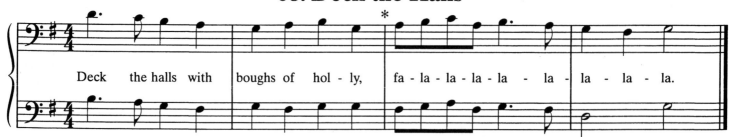

69. America the Beautiful

70. Angels We Have Heard on High

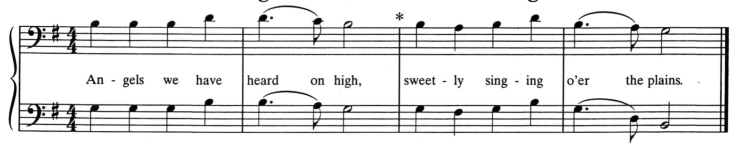

71. My Country 'Tis of Thee

72. Good King Wenceslas

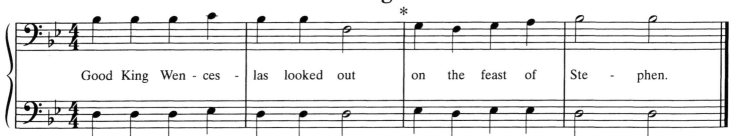

Good King Wen - ces - las looked out on the feast of Ste - phen.

73. Beethoven's Third Symphony

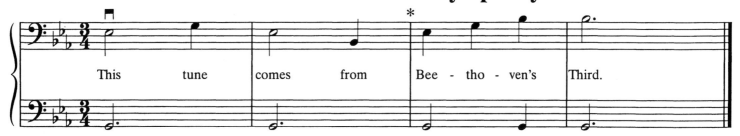

This tune comes from Bee - tho - ven's Third.

74. Where, Oh Where

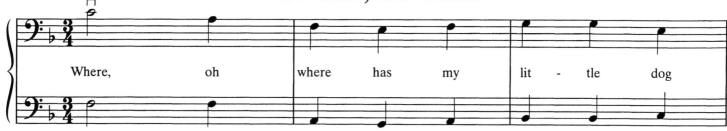

Where, oh where has my lit - tle dog

gone? Oh where, oh where can he be?

75. Do Re Mi

Do re do re do re mi. Fa mi fa mi re re do.

Fast Finger Action

76. D-A Finger Variation for Twinkle

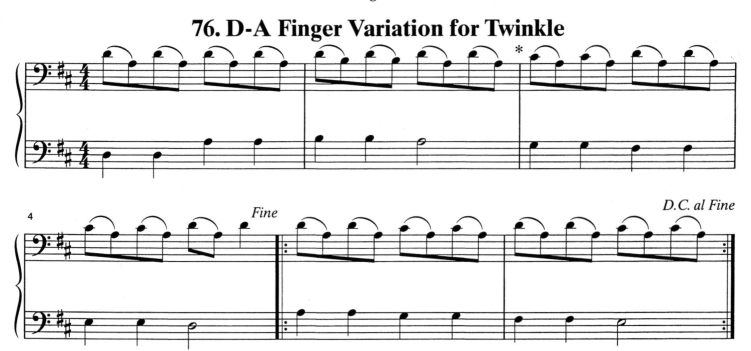

77. D-A-D-A Finger Variation for Twinkle